PoliticKu

The World Is in a Big Fucking Mess and I'm Writing Snotty Haiku About It:

A Mini-Guide to Everything That's Wrong

by Michelle Shy

Illustrations by John Crowther

Copyright © 2011 by Michelle Shy

Published by Michelle Shy

First edition 2011

Illustrations copyright by John Crowther

Cover design by Tatiana Vila.

Cover art by Tatiana Vila.

Cover image copyright CanStcokPhoto/rolffimages

Editing by Sandra de Helen

The following poems previously appeared in *SnarkyKu* by Michelle Shy: Gogyohka 3, Senryu 91, Senryu 152, Senryu 269, Senryu 413, Senryu 6, Senryu 133, Senry 153, Senryu 325, Senryu 434, Senryu 16, Senryu 138, Senryu 154, Senryu 328, Senryu 512, Senryu 21, Senryu 148, Senryu 219, Senryu 352, Senryu 515, Senryu 21, Senryu 148, Senryu 219, Senryu 352, Senryu 515, Senryu 40, Senryu 149, Senryu 238, Senryu 404, Senryu 518, Senryu 90, Senryu 150, Senryu 245, Senryu 409, Senryu 792. The following poems previously appeared in *DogKu* by Michelle Shy: Haiku 24, Senryu 181, Senryu 204

ISBN-13: 978-1467978491 | ISBN-10: 1467978493

"Michelle Shy's senryus *have a combination of intense impact, incisive commentary and poetic craft that sets her work apart."*

"Reading it is like eating Oreo cookies—hard to stop."

"...intelligent, funny, entertaining and moving."

"This delightful book will have you posting some of its haikus on your refrigerator and sending others to friends and enemies—especially enemies."

"Once I started, I couldn't put it down. I kept thinking I will just read one more *into the night."*

"Please, do not deprive yourself of another week of life lived without this gem on your coffee table."

"You'll laugh; you'll cry! You will smile at these bittersweet witticisms."

"...revels deliriously in its love of language and sense of parody, all the while exposing the ridiculous ways in which we have chosen to treat each other and squander our potential."

.

THANKS

You know who you are.

CONTENTS

ILLUSTRATIONS

Senryu 400

Calling Carl Sagan
World is filled with ignorance
Please come back to life

Michelle Shy

UNEMPLOYMENT

It sucks

"Look on the bright side, pal, we happen to be cutting edge.
Unemployment is trending."

GOGYOHKA 3

Starbucks is posting

Calories

Who cares?

I need Starbucks

To post jobs

TWITTERHAIKU 17

I was a teacher.

Laid off. Cancer. COBRA gone.

Eighteen months. Homeless.

SENRYU 327

Worked thirty-five years

My pension plan was secure

Then Citibank failed

SENRYU 870

I was in the cult

Worked at Apple, bought Apples

Outsourced to China

KYOKA 2

I'm above the fray

College degree, middle class

You proles gripe too much…

GM lays off white-collars

Oops. Hi, there, fellow wage slaves.

TANKA 78

Maybe if I walk

One hundred miles till I drop

Tongue swollen from thirst

I can put it out of mind

That I have no job

TANKA 64

Once upon a time

I was *trés* legitimate

They gave me access

To secure buildings with guards

I wore suits and heels

TANKA 65

It seems so long now

Since I was a real person

Could get my hair cut

Got a paycheck every month

Another lifetime ago

SENRYU 759

Try to remember

When I could afford latte

Like a real person

TWITTERHAIKU 77

Baby in ER

Sniffles turned to pneumonia

Mom was uninsured

SENRYU 824

My ex dot-com boss

Has homes in New York and Cannes

I have a small shack

SENRYU 515

Since the dot-com bust,

Bald, fat, Harvard MBAs

Fill me with boiled rage.

TANKA 6

Broke college student

Evicted from apartment

Senior citizen

Her home foreclosed by the bank

Cuts keener fifty years on

TANKA 9

Evicted once more

Years ago from apartment

Now from my own home

But from this wrinkle in time

I've no way to recover

SENRYU 863

Occupied with work?

No. I'm laid off. My new job:

Occupy Wall Street.

THE ECONOMY

"I got an idea, let's play house. You be the single
mommy with a sub-prime mortgage and I'll
be your banker and foreclose."

TWITTERHAIKU 18

No job...can't buy stuff...

Don't buy stuff...businesses close...

No jobs. Great system.

SENRYU 288

My art or my rent

Why must I choose only one?

Capitalism

SENRYU 796

Dreamed I had to choose

Letting my kitties drown or

Having a career

SENRYU 864

My broker tells me

European market's strong

Then Greece collapses

SENRYU 328

Family budget

Argue, shout, cry, yell, cry, blame

Let's skip it this month

SENRYU 325

Stealing is not right

Twenty-percent interest rate

Isn't that stealing?

SENRYU 91

Stealing is not right

Neg-am mortgage loans

Seem to be okay

TWITTERHAIKU 40

Stealing is not right.

Loaf of bread: six years. Bank fraud:

Ooooh, a big ol' fine.

TWITTERHAIKU 89

We got new schoolbooks

Three kids per book. Not Mali

East Oakland, Cali

EQUALITY INTERLUDE

SENRYU 138

Sorry, we don't hire

Blacks, older women, homos.

Why: free enterprise.

SENRYU 150

No, I'm serious.

We only hire white men

And hot, young, blond chicks.

Michelle Shy

EMPLOYMENT

It sucks too if you have to work for shit corporate bosses.

"Hey, I got a good one. Let's tell 'em the latest hike in gas prices is tied to the rising divorce rate in Ulan Bator."

SENRYU 415

Shall I be truthful?

Sarcastic? Rude? Seductive?

Job interview prep

DOGGEREL 8

Dreaded crazy boss man

Among the things I hate

Spreadsheet and project plan

Sarcasm when I'm late

Your crappy, borked LAN

Being in by eight

TANKA 132

These are the bad things

Which destroy my self-respect:

Spreadsheets, tedium,

Lies, quotas, petty tyrants...

You, crazy boss-hole.

SENRYU 318

Got to keep my job

Fucking psycho boss lady

Who treats me like shit

SENRYU 434

My boss's baby

Stupid, ugly and smells bad.

I say, "Oh, he's cute!"

SENRYU 518

When my boss gets rich

I should be happy for him

Although I'm still poor

SENRYU 472

You grab what you want

I get what I can scrounge for

That does not seem fair

SENRYU 867

Far East sales VP

Peering at a huge world map:

"Hey, where is Japan?"

SENRYU 868

Microsoft dude claims,

"We always release on time."

...like Windows 7?

SENRYU 869

My boss at Apple

Tells me I can't come to work

With my Blackberry

SENRYU 871

Working for Macy's

Emergency 3 a.m.

"Where's the Gaga bras?"

SENRYU 872

Hundred bucks per hour

Consultant sits in meeting

Playing Sudoku

SENRYU 873

We get free massage,

Free lattes, lunch and dinner.

Twenty-hour days.

SENRYU 508

"Be honest with me

How am I doing?" "Oh, fine."

Three weeks hence: "You're fired."

SENRYU 487

Worked two years nonstop.

While I was in surgery,

Boss griped, "She's slacking."

SENRYU 458

While drafting documents

To fire him, she told him thus:

"Your job is secure."

SENRYU 859

Amazon dot-com

Work eighteen-hour days, then

 "Don't let the door hit you…"

TANKA 125

Leaving Seattle

Passed the Amazon building

Rolled down my window

Stuck my head out and shouted

"Adios, Motherfuckers!"

EQUALITY INTERLUDE

"Take it from me, One Crooked Feather, give these illegals an inch and pretty soon they'll take a mile."

MICROPOEM 39

Fifteen-year-old Native kid

Dies in jail

Alcohol poisoning

SENRYU 198

Will this idea work?

Give the U.S. back to the

Indigenous peeps

SENRYU 625

Eavesdropped in L.A:

"Mexicans do the dishes.

That's as it should be."

ENTREPRENEURSHIP

Startups are just corporations with worse benefits and longer hours.

DEMENTED DIALOG 55

CEO: Don't invite the VP of marketing to any more marketing meetings.

DEMENTED DIALOG 33

VP: Why are there seven versions of the org chart that you send to seven different executives?

CEO: I demand flexibility.

DEMENTED DIALOG 30

CEO: Can you come to an executive meeting?

Me: What is the agenda?

CEO: We're just gonna talk about stuff.

DEMENTED DIALOG 60

VP: This project has too quick a turnaround time to bother with managing it. We are going to just DO it.

DEMENTED DIALOG 62

July

- CEO: Me, you and Joan are on the executive team.

August

- CEO: Joan is an idiot; Maurice and I are on the executive team.

September

- CEO: I fired Maurice. Me, you and George are on the executive team.

December

- CEO: George is a sociopath. Me, Paul and you are on the executive team.

January

- CEO: Cam, Leonard, Eliot, Sam, Joan, George and Paul all quit.

- VP: Maybe you should let someone else be involved in the interview process.

- CEO: I reserve the right to make all hiring decisions.

DEMENTED DIALOG 45

CEO: Why, why, why did you show the company president the new org chart where I demoted him to VP? Now he will want to TALK about it. Shit! I don't have time to talk to him.

DEMENTED DIALOG 46

CEO: We're building a company.

Reporter: Then why is everyone working for free?

CEO: Oh, I guess we're building a nonprofit.

Reporter: Then why don't you have 501 (c) 3 or any charitable programs?

CEO: We're building a company.

Reporter: You have no capital, no revenue streams and no budget.

CEO: You don't believe in the dream.

DEMENTED DIALOG 49

Board Member: Why haven't I been invited to the board meetings?

CEO: Stop stalking me. It is inappropriate for a 50-year-old man to be so obsessed with meeting a 35-year-old woman.

DEMENTED DIALOG 22

CEO: Mike just resigned. He had no reason to leave.
Satan tempted him.

DEMENTED DIALOG 14

VP: How did your interview with your potential new
hire go?

CEO: He did not flirt with me. He must be gay.

DEMENTED DIALOG 15

CEO: After the meeting, he sent me an article about our
industry...he sent it after business hours...he must be in
love with me.

DEMENTED DIALOG 29

CEO: We are building a global company. I am the only
one who can be on the board of directors because I
can't trust anyone else.

DEMENTED DIALOG 27

Business Partner: Can we discuss why the launch
strategy has changed three times this year?

CEO: NO, NO, NO! This is my company! MINE!

DEMENTED DIALOG 5

Cofounder: How many shares were issued, and who got what?

CEO: That is none of your business.

Cofounder: We've been business partners for three years, and you didn't tell me you had issued the stock?

CEO: I was mad at you because you didn't clean up my dirty dishes.

DEMENTED DIALOG 6

CEO: Don't tell Beth we don't have a platform.

Me: Why would I lie to a business partner?

CEO: It's called "managing information."

- So don't tell Allan we have no funding.

- Oh, don't tell Chris five partners are suing us.

- Don't tell Paul I am fucking our lead investor.

- Don't tell Martin we are firing him.

- Don't copy Kim on that memo.

VP to CEO: You have so much integrity.

DEMENTED DIALOG 21

CEO: We have our first investor.

Me: When do we get the money?

CEO: He is waiting for other investors to come in first.

DEMENTED DIALOG 10

CEO: Meet our new big-time investor.

New Big-Time Investor: I will help you sign up for this program to make $100 a day working from home.

CULTURAL INTERLUDE

"I'm tired of them whining liberals saying violent rhetoric is causin' violence. People just ain't influenced so easy by words and images."

I cry to think that our species' highly developed communication skills have devolved to the point where corporate communications, commercials and trash entertainment turn our brains to oatmeal.

SENRYU 862

Viva Las Vegas

False Paris, false Rome, false breasts

False hopes of lucre

TANKA 100

Sam went to Vegas

Bought me a baseball cap

Shiny pink glitter

Gold letters declare

"I won a HUNDRED dollars!!!!"

SENRYU 651

Watched late-night TV

After ten years in Peace Corps

Same shit Ginsu knives

TWITTERHAIKU 92B

I saw a movie

Such brilliant, unique story

Tits and car crashes

SENRYU 895

Hollywood dogma

Action hero plus hot chick

Solves the world's problems

SENRYU 894

Slice me up, doctor

My lips, my butt, they're all wrong

How much will it cost?

SENRYU 866

I want to grow up

Famous for being useless

Kim Kardashian

SENRYU 896

School-kid's career goal

Don't want to learn anything

Want to have groupies

SENRYU 898

My dreams, my life goals?

The same car as Beyoncé

Paris Hilton's shoes

SENRYU 892

Cheer my football team

When they win Super Bowl rings

I get...um...nothing

SENRYU 893

I love Michael Vick

Don't care if he tortures dogs

In his private life

SENRYU 897

I'm drinking Cuervo

Hot chicks will swarm around me

...till I puke on them

SENRYU 899

But, Mom, that man said

Instant breakfast is good food,

That man on TV

SENRYU 269

Believe me, believe

It will happen soon, the bliss

Just keep donating

OTHER CRAP JOBS

I've been fired from 79 random jobs.

SENRYU 792

Fired from my job

'Cause my apron was wrinkled:

High School for the Blind

TANKA 141

Smell of lemons

Stimulate memory

Stifling

Slaving

Sunshine Biscuits factory

DEMENTED DIALOG 26

Me: Stop patting me on the ass with your file handle.

He: OK.

Me: Also, stop patting me on the ass with your lathe wrench.

SENRYU 874

Here's a job for you.

You do have a college degree?

Chop up these onions.

SENRYU 875

Standing on Broad Street

Clicking a little counter

When cars hit potholes

SENRYU 875

Ten minutes in line

At the time clock—to punch out

For a half-hour lunch

SENRYU 877

Honey, you're working

Too fast, too efficiently

Makes the rest look bad

SENRYU 878

See these documents?

Move them all to this table

Then move them back here

SENRYU 879

Investigated

But they pay minimum wage

Phone sex lines

NOTREALLYPOEM 8

Peggy folds neckties

For minimum wage

When she needs some extra cash

The boss lets her blow him

SENRYU 883

Sarah cuts neckties

"You don't need a union, dear,

I'll take care of you

SENRYU 884

Glenda packs neckties

At lunch, wiping tears away

With designer silk

SENRYU 880

You can't wear glasses

While you're doing pole dances

Glasses aren't sexy

SENRYU 881

Welcome to Howdy

Would you like a Frute Fluffee

With your burger, sir?

SENRYU 882

Boss, can I get trained

To run the milling machine?

No, girls are too dumb

SENRYU 885

Pluck all these chickens

Don't bother to wash your hands

This is the rush hour

SENRYU 886

Tin cans slice my hands

Both wrists are weak from packing

Peach-canning plant

GOGYOHKA 5

Head Start school

In the kitchen

Retired marine sergeant

Steals meat from the kids

Fills up his home freezer

DEMENTED DIALOG 68

Actual section from instructor's training manual for Comedy Traffic School:

"Do not make jokes about the following:

- **Drunk driving**
- **The court system**
- **Cops**
- **Traffic laws**
- **The stupidity of traffic laws**
- **Car insurance**
- **Road workers**
- **The Department of Transportation**
- **Road rage**
- **Taking responsibility for your own driving errors**
- **Elderly drivers**
- **Women drivers**
- **Teenage drivers**
- **Chinese drivers**
- **Elderly Chinese women taxi drivers**
- **Politics**
- **Sex**
- **Religion**
- **Gruesome car accidents**
- **Having your guts chopped in half in an airliner crash"**

When my students turned in their evaluation forms, they all said, "She was NOT funny!"

LIMERICK 11

Met a rich man at the Met

Wants me to be his sex pet

Told my current honey

"I'm doing this for the money

To pay off your Julliard debt"

EQUALITY INTERLUDE

SENRYU 596

You're too old, too tall

Too brunet or too ethnic

Your boobs are too small

SENRYU 133

You know I love you.

So why do you force me to

Punch you, kick you again?

SENRYU 352

Please, I'm begging you

Make me feel like a woman

So stupid, so weak

TANKA 58

When I was eighteen

I could be the best

Now I have learned

Too smart, too pretty

Is such a threat

TANKA 59

People feel threatened

When I excel

So I quit

Trying

At all

TANKA 28

Everyone's lips

Are exactly the same

Twenty-year-olds'

Seventy-year-olds'

Botox Barbies

SENRYU 381

West Hollywood Heights

Showing off their breast implants

Fifteen-year-old girls

TANKA 56

Asked the doctor why

He wrecked my breast reconstruction

He said, "You're an old lady

No one will look at your chest

Anyway"

U.S. FOREIGN POLICY

A Day In Afghanistan

"Go figure, Joe, every year for the past hunnerd years
they've given some dude a million bucks to reward him
for bringin' peace to the world."

TWITTERHAIKU 94

The world is a mess

Dogs following troops around

In Afghanistan

TWITTERHAIKU 54

Buy me a diamond

Mined by slaves, drenched in tears, starved

It shines more that way

SENRYU 905

Go on, take that vote

If you vote Palestine in

We withdraw our cash

SENRYU 904

Need to learn torture?

School of the Americas

Tuition rebate

RENGA 4

Korea, China,

Vietnam, Egypt, Haiti,

Thailand, Cuba, Laos,

El Salvador, Honduras,

Panama, Macedonia,

Colombia, Peru,

Dominicana, Israel, Laos,

Congo, Nicaragua, Chad

Haiti, Cambodia, Iraq,

Afghanistan, Pakistan,

Yemen, Cote d'Ivoire,

Libya, Afghanistan,

Iraq, Haiti,

Saudi Arabia, Iraq,

Haiti, Libya, Grenada,

Persian Gulf, Iraq,

Iran, Pakistan, Timor,

Salvador, Chile,

Angola, Bolivia,

Chile asesinado.

SENRYU 903

Here come U.S. troops

Get rid of your dictator

Install ours instead

CULTURAL INTERLUDE: LET'S STOP KIDDING OURSELVES

SENRYU 153

We are the chosen

God likes us better than you

But don't be jealous.

TWITTERHAIKU 100

Why am I laid off?

I'm white and American.

I deserve better.

SENRYU 900

Rape, assassinate

Interfere in elections

We are the good guys

SENRYU 901

Love your country

Does that mean hate all others?

Does it mean don't think?

SENRYU 127

Eminent domain

All Latin America

Is OUR property

SENRYU 164

Cuba's very bad!

Free college education

For all citizens.

SENRYU 6

Oh, Fidel is bad!

Yet they have more doctors per

Capita than we.

SENRYU 235

Please speak pleasantly

Don't make me feel discomfort

Don't mention Gitmo

"Okay, you hate America, dude. So why don't you go
be homeless someplace better?"

TANKA 148

"They" torture suspects

"We" enhance interrogate

"They" are terrorists

"We" are fighting for freedom

May God bless America

SENRYU 149

What would Jesus say?

Six of ten Evangelists

Say torture's OK

ELECTORAL POLITICS

The Big Lie

"How the heck do we play Democrats and Republicans?
There's no good guys."

You think we can fix anything simply by voting for the guy with (D) after his name who gets at least $3,500,000 in campaign contributions from Wall Street?

SENRYU 476

Admire the leader

Who speaks so persuasively

But then does nothing

DEMENTED DIALOG 24

Change we need: If you don't have enough money to buy health insurance, we'll fine you.

SENRYU 860

Barack, Hillary

Praise Libya demonstrators

Damn Occupiers

SENRYU 322

The same old, old shit

We do fall for it always

And over again

SENRYU 404

Isn't that dandy?

It's no longer called a lie.

"Conserving the Truth"

SENRYU 888

Meet Mister Perry

He likes executing folks

Thinks it's quite a gas

SENRYU 887

Laugh, motherfucker

As we die from no health care

You'll get yours real soon

SENRYU 889

Googled Herman Cain

Top search result by far:

"Idiot jackass"

SENRYU 890

Then we have Bachmann

Attributes swine flu outbreaks

To Jimmy Carter

SENRYU 891

Under Obama

More "illegals" deported

Than under George Bush

SENRYU 413

Can you go to Yale

And still be an idiot?

Yes, I'm sure of it.

TWITTERHAIKU 37

Man with pea-size brain

Functioning civil servant

George Double You Bush

SENRYU 398

We arrest small thieves

And appoint the great thieves

To public office

{Paraphrasing Aesop}

EQUALITY INTERLUDE

SENRYU 146

You've got twenty years

Background; but yet, we didn't

Think you'd be so old.

SENRYU 148

Miss California

With silicon boobs, worries

About gay marriage

SENRYU 245

A marriage should be

Between one man and woman

Plus his mistresses

SENRYU 219

Cheating, wife beating,

Incest, child abuse, divorce.

Fine. Just don't be gay.

CLASS SOCIETY: PRESENTING THE 1 PERCENT

"I'd love to get involved as an activist in a good cause, but after social obligations, the gym, ceramics classes, and shopping, I have no discretionary time left."

SENRYU 430

They say, "Good luck with that"

Don't take them at their word

They mean, "Fuck off and die"

HOLLYWOOD SENRYU 638

I donate some bucks

To the homeless shelter. BUT

Clear them off MY street

SENRYU 326

I can ignore you

If I dehumanize you

I can't see your pain

TWITTERHAIKU 35

Wearing Gucci shoes

She carefully steps over

George begging for change

SENRYU 425

Have you heard from Rabb?

Now that he's a millionaire

He won't speak to me

SENRYU 152

Come visit my home

Chat of art, foreign travel

Not the recession

SENRYU 624

L.A. distortion

Dude has five full-time servants

Complaining he's broke

TANKA 75

Malibu

Fixer

Zero-lot-line

Mobile home

One million dollars

TWITTERHAIKU 21

Recession tactics

No French nails or hair streaking

Fire the housekeeper

SENRYU 143

This wine is too tart

You complain, yet some people

Have no food to eat

TANKA 87

My two neighbor friends

La Beatriz d'arriba

Studies for her MBA

La Beatriz d'abajo

Husband keeps her locked inside

SENRYU 134

Would you give up one

Of your designer ball gowns

To feed a stranger?

SENRYU 409

My rich mom and dad

Sent me to Ivy League schools.

I'm a self-made man.

SENRYU 408

A "world-class" climber

Reached the top of Everest

He needed six Sherpas' help

SENRYU 330

You have lung cancer:

You poor thing…you got laid off:

The blame lies with you.

TWITTERHAIKU 90

You must deserve it

It must be your fault; you're bad

That's why you're poor

SENRYU 329

I drink fine champagne.

We were once friends, but no more:

You can't afford wine.

SENRYU 902

Election reform

Reasonable democracy

One dollar, one vote

SENRYU 399

A capitalist

The title you give yourself

Real name: "bloodsucker"

{Paraphrasing Malcolm X)

SENRYU 365

I'm losing my home.

We'll be living in a tent.

She responds, "How cool!"

CULTURAL INTERLUDE: RELATIONSHIPS

"They've been rescued from extinction by developers in the jungles of Peru and brought here, where they've been given the chance to maintain their indigenous lifestyle."

Human interaction becomes commoditized.

SENRYU 516

Read into my heart

Promises, my deepest dreams

Then cheat me, use me

SENRYU 432

Do you want world peace?

Yes, me too. So, join my cult;

Give me all your cash.

SENRYU 371

Mind your own business

This child is my property

I can beat this child

TANKA 45

Hot summer day

Three neighbors' open windows

Car chase on TV

Glass jars clinking, recycle

Young child hit with leather belt

SENRYU 238

His wife has left him

He doesn't really miss her

Anyone will do

SENRYU 355

"You're no longer hot."

"Then go find a younger wife."

"No, you have money."

SENRYU 261

Susan Boyle's a meme

No, she's Simon's new product

No, she's a person

SENRYU 512

The more men I fuck

The more powerful I am.

Wait...it doesn't work.

SENRYU 129

So much doggy-style

So little human contact

No intimacy

THE ENVIRONMENT

What's there to say about this that those damn granolas haven't been saying for years?

TANKA 107

I, among the few,

Watched the last glacier calving

Otherworldly blue

Before it melted forever

In the final days on Earth

TANKA 18

The ocean

Empty

Devoid of aquatic life

Earth has no fish

2020

TANKA 106

Dead baby seagull

Buried in beach sand

Floppy neck, but eyes still bright

I dug him up

But the waves buried him again

TANKA 1

Tearing your limbs off

Eating you from the inside

Call me Pine Beetle

And you are dying Pine

Your red death fills the mountains

SENRYU 671

Highway 17

What was once a marshy hill

Gouged by strip mining

MICROPOEM 38

Antelope grazing ground

No antelope

On the road

Two dead

News Break:
Did you know it is legal for people to eat roadkill in several states, including Illinois, Texas and West Virginia?

TANKA 38

Dead creatures, blood, guts

One by one on the roadside

So few creatures left

Soon we'll drive the empty road

No creatures left in the world

SENRYU 577

Goodbye, life on earth

With the oceans depleted

We are all dying

HAIKU 13

Zombie pine beetles

Global warming's viral plague

Ravish forest life

DEATHKU 12

Baiji dolphin. Gone.

None could be found in Yangtze.

Species is extinct.

DEATHKU 40

Baby bird suffers

Is this what life will look like

Emboweled in Hell?

EQUALITY INTERLUDE

"A new study says the noise they make isn't just chatter. They can actually communicate simple concepts to each other.":

I just don't think you're fully human if you can watch a helpless-but-feeling-and-thinking creature suffer.

SENRYU 861

Viva Las Vegas

Chained white tigers performing

For drunken, rich pigs

MICROPOEM 35

Barred, caged prison

Cousin

Why are you doing these things?

It hurts

Chimp

TANKA 146

Baby raccoon

Loving eyes ringed in black Kohl

Are you my mom?

No, little kit, I'm human

One of my kind killed your mom

TANKA 108

Up Avalanche Gulch

Lovely, healthy coyote

Joyous dog-creature

Rifle shot in her front leg

She bled out on a snow bank

TANKA 109

Walked to her body

Still warm

Yet no life

Blood pouring out

The same color as mine

TANKA 110

Gorgeous coyote

Shot to death just for fun

Nearby, the small pup

Whom she was trying to shield

Also dead

TANKA 111

Found the shell casing

Bunch of assholes in an ATV

Followed their tire tracks

To their house

Burned it down

TANKA 112

All afternoon

We looked for a live one

To make the balance

But there was no live one

And no balance

TANKA 96

Tokyo

Not one cigarette butt on the street

Schoolgirls are safe at 3 a.m.

Taiji

Dolphins are murdered

TANKA 33

Small cages

Giraffes imprisoned since birth

Punished for no crime

Now executed in the gas chamber

To help the zoo's budget

TANKA 17

Biting and ripping

She devours what was his body

Temple of the soul

But no matter

He's just a veal calf

SENRYU 769

Love your pretty face

Intelligent eyes, soft hair

I'll shoot and stuff you

SENRYU 711

Grizzly bear spotted

Twenty miles away. I'm scared

Hunters will shoot me

SENRYU 606

It doesn't matter

If we torture monkeys, pigs,

For they can't do math

TWITTERHAIKU 24

Share the earth with all

Humans, animals all

We die without them

DEATHKU 13

Who the hell told you

That you have a right to kill

And mount our stuffed heads?

TWITTERHAIKU 26

Humans made a mess

And only we can fix it

Let's stop extinction

TANKA 137

Two teenagers

Orange kitten

Rope around neck

Swinging him

Smashing his soft body flat

SENRYU 147

No business of yours

If I torture this kitty.

I'm not hurting you.

SENRYU 181

I don't want to live

In an empty, barren world

Devoid of species

SENRYU 202

He dumped her body

By the roadside. That's OK,

She was "just a wolf."

SENRYU 203

She was a Lobo

F836, rare, threatened,

Killed by a poacher

SENRYU 204

Why all this hatred?

All animals share the earth.

We all eat, love, play.

SENRYU 242

What is luxury?

Skins of tortured animals

Juice from stifled moths

END GAME

"Okay, we agree, revolution, but if we're successful
let's hope nobody ever has to hear any more of that
talk about change."

Well, what are you going to do?

SENRYU 360

My dad's parting words

As I'm leaving for college:

Don't go to protests

SENRYU 865

Occupy Wall Street

Keep gnawing from the inside

Belly of the beast

SENRYU 665

East 14th billboard

"Honky Imperialists

Out of East Oakland"

SENRYU 666

Cruising East 14th

I spot this huge graffiti:

"Mao More Than Ever"

SENRYU 614

There is disorder

Great chaos under Heaven

This is excellent

{Paraphrasing Mao)

SENRYU 172

Power of freedom

Is greater than powers of

Oppressors, tyrants

{Paraphrasing Malcolm X)

SENRYU 173

Nobody can give you

Freedom, equality, rights

But you can take them

{Paraphrasing Malcolm X)

SENRYU 175

A man who stands for

Nothing nothing nothing…will

Fall for anything

{Paraphrasing Malcolm X)

SENRYU 177

You can't separate

Peace from freedom…you can't have

Peace with slavery

{Paraphrasing Malcolm X)

SENRYU 616 *for Jeanne*

We're working so hard

Making justice in the world

Still more work remains

SENRYU 513

Torture me, break me,

Rip me apart. Even then

I'll still speak the truth.

...AND JUST TO BE ANNOYING

SENRYU 442
Oh, yeah, you disdain
My simple analysis
Yet I am correct

"Well of course it's just my opinion, but it's the damn truth!"

MICROPOEM 14

Mixed marriage

She's so Zen

He's Battle in Seattle

MICROPOEM 16

Mixed marriage

She's Amnesty International

He's CIA

MICROPOEM 29

Mixed marriage

Black woman

Hell's Angels guy

MICROPOEM 10

Mixed marriage

Reality TV show-runner

Solo performance artist

MICROPOEM 2

Mixed marriage

Nicotine-stained fingers

Wheat grass and brown rice

MICROPOEM 17

Mixed marriages

So difficult to sustain

Men and women

MICROPOEM 30

Mixed marriages

Liz Taylor

Michelle Shy

INTERVIEW QUESTIONS

For Amy, Bill, John, Keith, Lawrence and Rachel to ask me

Q: George W. Bush?
A: War criminal.

Q: Dick Cheney?
A: War criminal.

Q: Condoleezza Rice?
A: War criminal.

Q: David Lesar?
A: Bourgeois pig. And war criminal.

Q: The guy who runs Bank of America?
A: Pig-fucking motherfucker. And give me my home back, you bastard.

A: Herman Cain?
B: Comprador bourgeois.

Q: Rick Perry?
A: Looks like a human, but no soul resides within.

Q: Healthcare reform of 2010?
A: What?

Q: Republican Party?
A: Wall Street.

Q: Democratic Party?
A: Wall Street.

Q: Wall Street?
A: *Halls of Congress.*

Q: President Obama?
A: "Change We Need"—oops—"Spare Change Wall Street Needs."

Q: Occupy Movement?
A: Amazing.

Q: Michael Moore?
A: I sent him a marriage proposal.

Q: Cornel West?
A: See Michael Moore, above.

Q: Steve Jobs?
A: Ginsu knives, only with cooler packaging.

Q: George Clooney?
A: I sent him a marriage proposal too.

If you liked this book...

...please leave me a review and
rating on Amazon. Thanks.

Did you have trouble reading this book?

Was the formatting OK? If not, please let me know at
http:michelleshy.com/contact-me. What device,
what operating system or what reader do
you use? Portrait or landscape? Thank
you. Your input will help me fix
problems with the book.

ABOUT THE AUTHOR

I am a comedian, performance artist, actor, screenwriter, filmmaker and author because a career counselor told me I'd never be able to hold down a straight gig. This prediction was accurate: I have been fired from 79 normal jobs.

My pets: 12 cats, seven dogs, four birds, two fish, two lizards and one rabbit. Most of these pets are dead and reside in plastic containers in the back closet. Those that are alive reside in the middle of my bed. I hope to get two more dogs tomorrow. Oh, and two goats.

If I weren't so gorgeous, you would think I am a huge pain in the butt because I lie so much.

SnarkyKu, my first book of haiku, has an average reader rating of 5 stars.

My 79 previous jobs include: machinist, welder, tool & die maker, document shredder, fast food waitress, software engineer, hardware engineer, product marketing, shoe salesman, pants salesman, product manager, field marketing, executive management consultant, process re-engineering consultant, project manager, engineering manager, program manager, film festival director, envelope stuffer, chicken plucker, stripper, pothole counter, necktie folder, reporter, chief operations officer, cardboard box folder, glass bottle inspector, vice president of a corporate division, ticket booth jockey, dishwasher, cookie packer, life coach, comedy traffic school instructor, telephone exchange operator, chef specializing in Top Ramen with one egg and no garnish...oh, and a few more.

Several of my screenplays—with elements of insanity—are under discussions with producers.

Sign up for my mailing list
for announcements of new
books.

My web site

Buy my books on
Amazon.com.

Follow me on Twitter.

PoliticKu mugs, buttons and T-shirts at <u>Cafe Press</u>

CONTRIBUTORS

Illustrations by John Crowther

Cover design by Tatiana Vila

Cover art by Tatiana Vila

Editing by Sandra de Helen

Copy editing by **Eric Althoff**

Author's photograph by Travis Sterner; makeup by Illusions by Melanie

ALSO BY MICHELLE SHY

AVAILABLE NOW AT YOUR FAVORITE ETAILER:

SnarkyKu

Snotty, mean, sarcastic, grouchy, grumpy, crabby, cranky, hateful little poems

DogKu

Snappy little *senryu* about and by animals

COMING SOON

AngstKu

Yeah, these are all about angst, depression, pain, death and misery. In other words, have fun reading! *AngstKu* will be available in January 2012.

MadKu

Written by the crazy cat lady down the street, these mini-poems are just plain nutsoid. *MadKu* will be available in February 2012.

Short Attention Span Poetry

Poems that, like little snacks, can be gobbled up in under a minute each.

News

Our sun will go supernova in March of the year 1,500,2012.

FREE DIRTY LITTLE SNEAK PEEK INTO MY NEXT BOOK

Angstku: These are all about angst, depression, pain, death, misery and REVENGE. Have fun reading.

Senryu 12
Why be sensible?
Life is tough and painful.
Just become a clown.

TwitterHaiku 58
So what if I wear
Black T-shirts, black pants, black shoes?
I am NOT depressed.

Senryu 121
Stop. I saw your tears.
Rather, felt them through the lids
Of my own closed eyes.

Senryu 136
My sixth-grade boyfriend
Dumped me in junior high school
For cheerleader Dawn.

Senryu 144
I put my words out
To the interstellar void
No echo comes back.